P9-DMX-467

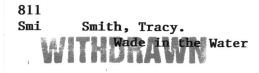
DATE DUE

WADE IN THE WATER

ALSO BY TRACY K. SMITH

Poetry
The Body's Question
Duende
Life on Mars

Memoir
Ordinary Light

Anthology
American Journal: Fifty Poems for Our Time

WADE IN THE WATER

POEMS

TRACY K. SMITH

GRAYWOLF PRESS

This publication is made possible, in part, by the voters of Minnesota through a
Minnesota State Arts Board Operating Support grant, thanks to a legislative appro-
priation from the arts and cultural heritage fund, and a grant from the Wells Fargo
Foundation. Significant support has also been provided by Target, the McKnight
Foundation, the Lannan Foundation, the Amazon Literary Partnership, and other
generous contributions from foundations, corporations, and individuals. To these
organizations and individuals we offer our heartfelt thanks.

Published by Graywolf Press
250 Third Avenue North, Suite 600
Minneapolis, Minnesota 55401

www.graywolfpress.org

Published in the United States of America

ISBN 978-1-55597-813-6 (cloth)
ISBN 978-1-55597-836-5 (paper)

2 4 6 8 10 9 7 5 3

Library of Congress Control Number: 2018947077

Cover design: Kyle G. Hunter

Cover art: Jie Zhao / Corbis News / Getty Images

for Tina

CONTENTS

III.

IV.

WADE IN THE WATER

I.

GARDEN OF EDEN

What a profound longing
I feel, just this very instant,
For the Garden of Eden
On Montague Street
Where I seldom shopped,
Usually only after therapy,
Elbow sore at the crook
From a handbasket filled
To capacity. The glossy pastries!
Pomegranate, persimmon, quince!
Once, a bag of black beluga
Lentils spilt a trail behind me
While I labored to find
A tea they refused to carry.
It was Brooklyn. My thirties.
Everyone I knew was living
The same desolate luxury,
Each ashamed of the same things:
Innocence and privacy. I'd lug
Home the paper bags, doing
Bank-balance math and counting days.
I'd squint into it, or close my eyes
And let it slam me in the face—
The known sun setting
On the dawning century.

THE ANGELS

Two slung themselves across chairs
Once in my motel room. Grizzled,
In leather biker gear. Emissaries
For something I needed to see.

I was worn down by an awful panic.
A wrenching in the gut, contortions.
They sat there at the table while I slept.
I could sense them, with a deck

Of playing cards between them.
To think of how they smelled, what
Comes to mind is rum and gasoline.
And when they spoke, though I couldn't,

I dared not look, I glimpsed how one's teeth
Were ground down almost to nubs.
Which makes me hope some might be
Straight up thugs, young, slim, raw,

Who bounce and roll with fearsome grace,
Whose very voices cause faint souls to quake.
—*Quake, then, fools, and fall away!*
—*What God do you imagine we obey?*

Think of the toil we must cost them,
One scaled perfectly to eternity.
And still, they come, telling us
Through the ages not to fear.

Just those two that once and never
Again for me since, though
There are—are there?—
Sightings, flashes, hints:

A proud tree in vivid sun, branches
Swaying in strong wind. Rain
Hurling itself at the roof. Boulders,
Mounds of earth mistaken for dead

Does, lions in crouch. A rust-stained pipe
Where a house once stood, which I
Take each time I pass it for an owl.
Bright whorl so dangerous and near.

My mother sat whispering with it
At the end of her life
While all the rooms of our house
Filled up with night.

HILL COUNTRY

He comes down from the hills, from

The craggy rock, the shrubs, the scrawny

Live oaks and dried-up junipers. Down

From the cloud-bellies and the bellies

Of hawks, from the caracaras stalking

Carcasses, from the clear, sun-smacked

Soundlessness that shrouds him. From the

Weathered bed of planks outside the cabin

Where he goes to be alone with his questions.

God comes down along the road with his

Windows unrolled so the twigs and hanging

Vines can slap and scrape against him in his jeep.

Down past the buck caught in the hog trap

That kicks and heaves, bloodied, blinded

By the whiff of its own death, which God—

Thank God—staves off. He downshifts,

Crosses the shallow trickle of river that only

Just last May scoured the side of the canyon

To rock. Gets out. Walks along the limestone

Bank. Castor beans. Cactus. Scat of last

Night's coyotes. Down below the hilltops,

He squints out at shadow: tree backing tree.

Dark depth the eye glides across, not bothering

To decipher what it hides. A pair of dragonflies

Mate in flight. Tiny flowers throw frantic color

At his feet. If he tries—if he holds his mind

In place and wills it—he can almost believe

In something larger than himself rearranging

The air. He squints at the jeep glaring

In bright sun. Stares awhile at patterns

The tall branches cast onto the undersides

Of leaves. Then God climbs back into the cab,

Returning to everywhere.

DEADLY

The holy thinks *Tiger*,
Then watches the thing
Wriggle, divide, stagger up
Out of the sea to rise on legs
And tear into the side
Of a loping gazelle,
Thinks *Man* and witnesses
The armies of trees and
Every nation of beast and
The wide furious ocean
And the epochs of rock
Tremble.

A MAN'S WORLD

He will surely take it out when you're alone
And let it dangle between you like a locket on a chain.
Like any world, it will flicker with lights that mean dwellings,
Traffic, a constellation of need. Tiny clouds will drag shadows
Across the plane. He'll grin watching you squint, deciphering
Rivers, borders, bridges arcing up from rock. He'll recite
Its history. How one empire swallowed another. How one
Civilization lasted 3,000 years with no word for *eternity*.
He'll guide your hand through the layers of atmosphere,
Teach you to tamper with the weather. Swinging it
Gently back and forth, he'll swear he's never shown it
To anyone else before.

THE WORLD IS YOUR BEAUTIFUL YOUNGER SISTER

Seeing her as seldom as you do, it doesn't change,
The ire, the shame, the fists you must remember

To smooth flat just thinking what they did,
What they promised, then took—those men

Who offered to pay, to keep, the clan of them
Lording it over the others like high school boys

And their kid brothers. Men with interests to protect,
And mute marble wives. Men who let her

Beam into their faces, watching her shoulders rise,
Her astonishing new breasts, making her believe

It was she who gave permission.
They plundered her youth, then moved on.

Those awful, awful men. The ones
Whose wealth is a kind of filth.

REALM OF SHADES

There was still a here, but that's not where we were, continually turning our backs to something unseen, speaking with just our eyes, getting on with work. What was our work? Our doors wouldn't lock. We rigged them, hung windows with sheets that broadcast our secrets after dark. People with weapons crept like thieves through their own houses. How did we feel? Like a canary cramped in a cage? Or the cat dying to know what the bird tastes like, swatting the rungs day after day, though the little hinged door never gives? No one hid. No one ran like a dog through the street. The moon traced its slow arc through the sky, drifting in and out of clouds that harbored nothing.

DRIVING TO OTTAWA

More and more now we slip
Into this tone of voice, the hush
Of people talking about someone
Who has just died, only
No one has died. We might be
Sisters, or old friends, or passengers
On the road to the airport. Once
I sat talking this way to a man
I'd only just met, while dawn
Floated up and turned all the white
Hills flush. The momentary kind
Of love two strangers share,
Pushing out those long sighs
And then rushing to fill the lungs
Again with weightless clear air.
Looking into the distance
Blotted out by hills that give way
Sometimes suddenly to silos
Or the teetering barns of a past
That's gone, but won't lie down
And let us grieve it.
                              The days
Are bright but cold. Our shadow
Spreads like ash across each road.
How much more will we bury
In the earth? How much
In this dark where the earth floats?

WADE IN THE WATER

for the Geechee Gullah Ring Shouters

One of the women greeted me.
I love you, she said. She didn't
Know me, but I believed her,
And a terrible new ache
Rolled over in my chest,
Like in a room where the drapes
Have been swept back. I love you,
I love you, as she continued
Down the hall past other strangers,
Each feeling pierced suddenly
By pillars of heavy light.
I love you, throughout
The performance, in every
Handclap, every stomp.
I love you in the rusted iron
Chains someone was made
To drag until love let them be
Unclasped and left empty
In the center of the ring.
I love you in the water
Where they pretended to wade,
Singing that old blood-deep song
That dragged us to those banks
And cast us in. I love you,
The angles of it scraping at
Each throat, shouldering past
The swirling dust motes
In those beams of light
That whatever we now knew
We could let ourselves feel, knew

To climb. O Woods—O Dogs—
O Tree—O Gun—O *Girl, run*—
O Miraculous Many Gone—
O Lord—O Lord—O Lord—
Is this love the trouble you promised?

II.

DECLARATION

He has

        sent hither swarms of Officers to harass our people

He has plundered our——

              ravaged our——

                            destroyed the lives of our——

taking away our——

              abolishing our most valuable——

and altering fundamentally the Forms of our——

*In every stage of these Oppressions We have Petitioned for
Redress in the most humble terms:*
                            *Our repeated
Petitions have been answered only by repeated injury.*

*We have reminded them of the circumstances of our emigration
and settlement here.*

        ——taken Captive
                  on the high Seas
                          to bear——

THE GREATEST PERSONAL PRIVATION

The greatest personal privation I have had to endure has been the want of either Patience or Phoebe—tell them I am never, if life is spared us, to be without both of them again.
—letter from Mary Jones to Elizabeth Maxwell regarding two of her slaves, 30 August 1849

1.

It is a painful and harassing business
Belonging to her. We have had trouble enough,
Have no comfort or confidence in them,

And they appear unhappy themselves, no doubt
From the trouble they have occasioned.
They could dispose of the whole family

Without consulting us—Father, Mother,
Every good cook, washer, and seamstress
Subject to sale. I believe Good shall be

Glad if we may have hope of the loss of trouble.
I remain in glad conscience, at peace with God
And the world! I have prayed for those people

Many, many, very many times.

2.

Much as I should miss Mother,
I have had trouble enough
And wish no more to be
Only waiting to be sent
Home in peace with God.

3.

In every probability
We may yet discover

The whole country
Will not come back

From the sale of parent
And child. So far

As I can see, the loss
Is great and increasing.

I know they have desired
We should not know

What was for our own good,
But we cannot be all the cause

Of all that has been done.

4.

We wish to act. We may yet.
But we have to learn what their

Character and moral conduct
Will present. We have it in

Contemplation to wait and see.
If good, we shall be glad; if

Evil, then we must meet evil
As best we can.

5.

Father, mother, son, daughter, man.
And if that family is sold:

Please—

We cannot—

Please—

We have got to—

Please—

The children—

Mother and Father and husband and—

All of you—

All—

I have no more—

How soon and unexpectedly cut off
Many, many, very many times.

UNWRITTEN

Neither do I think it would at all promote the slave's interest to lib-
erate him in his present degraded state.
— letter from Mary Jones to Charles Colcock Jones,
24 November 1829

Much as I should miss the mother, I am
Persuaded that we might come
To some understanding about a change
Of investment. I do not wish
To influence you in the least degree
Beyond your own convictions, nor
To have you subjected to inconveniences
(The loss of the services of a servant is great),
But for our own good we have to answer
For all that has happened. Please. All.

I WILL TELL YOU THE TRUTH ABOUT THIS,
I WILL TELL YOU ALL ABOUT IT

Carlisle, Pa. Nov 21 1864

Mr abarham lincon
I wont to knw sir if you please
whether I can have my son relest
from the arme   he is all the subport
I have now   his father is Dead
and his brother that wase all
the help I had   he has bean wonded
twise he has not had nothing to send me yet
now I am old and my head is blossaming
for the grave and if you do I hope
the lord will bless you and me
tha say that you will simpethise
withe the poor   he be long to the
eight rigmat colard troops
he is a sarjent
mart welcom is his name

Benton Barracks Hospital, St. Louis, Mo. September 3 1864

My Children

I take my pen in hand to rite you A few lines
to let you know that I have not Forgot you
be assured that I will have you if it cost me my life
on the 28th of the month 8 hundred White and
8 hundred blacke solders expects to start up
the river to Glasgow   when they Come
I expect to be with them and expect to get you
Both in return
                Your Miss Kaitty said that I tried
to steal you   You tell her from me that if she
meets me with ten thousand soldiers she will meet
Her enemy
                Give my love to all enquiring friends
tell them all that we are well

The morning was bitter cold.
It was freezing hard. I was
certain it would kill my sick child
to take him out in the cold. I told
the man in charge of the guard
that it would be the death of my boy.

I told him that my wife and children
had no place to go and that I
was a soldier of the United States.
He told me it did not make any difference.
He had orders to take all out of Camp.
He told my wife and family that if they

did not get up into the wagon he would
shoot the last one of them. My wife
carried her sick child in her arms.
The wind was blowing hard and cold
and having had to leave much of our
clothing when we left our master, my wife

with her little one was poorly clad. I followed
as far as the lines. At night I went in search.
They were in an old meeting house belonging
to the colored people. My wife and children
could not get near the fire, because
of the number of colored people huddling

by the soldiers. They had not received
a morsel of food during the whole day.
My boy was dead. He died directly
after getting down from the wagon.
Next morning I walked to Nicholasville.
I dug a grave and buried my child. I left

my family in the Meeting house—
where they still remain.

Nashville, Tenn. Aug 12th 1865

Dear Wife,

I am in earnis about you comeing
and that as Soon as possible

It is no use to Say any thing about any money
for if you come up here which I hope you will
it will be all wright as to the money matters

I want to See you and the Children very bad
I can get a house at any time I will Say the word
So you need not to fear as to that So come
wright on just as Soon as you get this

I want you to tell me the name of the baby
that was born Since I left

I am your affectionate Husband untill Death

Belair, Md. Aug 25th 1864

Mr president   It is my Desire to be free   to go to see my people
on the eastern shore   my mistress wont let me   you will please
let me know if we are free   and what i can do

Excellent Sir   My son went in the 54th regiment—

Sir, my husband, who is in Co. K. 22nd Reg't U.S. Cold Troops
(and now in the Macon Hospital at Portsmouth with a wound in his arm)
has not received any pay since last May and then only thirteen dollars—

Sir   We The Members of Co D of the 55th Massechusetts vols
Call the attention of your Excellency to our case—

for instant look & see
that we never was freed yet
Run Right out of Slavery
In to Soldiery & we
hadent nothing atall &
our wifes & mother most all of them
is aperishing all about & we
all are perishing our self—

i am willing to bee a soldier and serve my time
faithful like a man but i think it is hard to bee
poot off in such dogesh manner as that—

Will you see that the colored men fighting now
are fairly treated. You ought to do this,
and do it at once, Not let the thing run along
meet it quickly and manfully. We poor oppressed ones
appeal to you, and ask fair play—

So Please if you can do any good for us do it
in the name of God—

Excuse my boldness but pleas—

30

your reply will settle the matter and will be appreciated,
by, a colored man who, is willing to sacrifice his son
in the cause of Freedom & Humanity—

I have nothing more to say
hoping that you will lend a listening ear
to an umble soldier
I will close—

Yours for Christs sake—

(i shall hav to send this with out a stamp
for I haint money enough to buy a stamp)

Clarksville, Tenn. Aug 28th 1865

Dear husband,

I guess you would like to know the reason why
that I did not come when you wrote for
and that is because I hadnot the money
and could not get it   and if you will
send me the money or come after me
I will come   they sent out
Soldiers from here After old Riley   and they
have got him in Jale   and one of his Sons
and they have his brother Elias here
in Jale   dear husband If you are coming after me
I want you to come before it Get too cold

Florence, Ala. December 7th 1866

Dear sir   I take the pleashure of writing you
A fue lins hoping that I will not ofende you
by doing so   I was raised in your state
and was sold from their when I was 31 years olde
left wife one childe Mother Brothers and sisters
My wife died about 12 years agoe and ten years
agoe I made money And went back and bought
My olde Mother and she lives with me

Seven years agoe I Maried again and commence
to by Myself and wife for two thousande dollars and
last Christmas I Made the last pay ment and I have
made Some little Money this year and I wish
to get my Kinde All with me and I will take it
as a Greate favor if you will help me to get them

My dear sister   I write you this letter to let you no
I am well   I ask of you in this letter to go and take
my boy from my wif as sh is not doing write by him
take him and keep him until I come home   if sh is
not willing to gave him up go and shoe this letter   it is
my recust for you to have him   I doe not want her
to have my child with another man   I would lik
for my child to be raised well   I will be hom next fall
if I live   a solder stand a bad chanc but if god spars me
I will be home

I am 60 odd years of age—

I am 62 years of age next month—

I am about 65 years of age—

I reckon I am about 67 years old—

I am about 68 years of age—

I am on the rise of 80 years of age—

I am 89 years old—

I am 94 years of age—

I don't know my exact age—

I am the claimant in this case. I have testified before you
two different times before—

I filed my claim I think first about 12 years ago—

I am now an applicant for a pension,
because I understand
that all soldiers are entitled to a pension—

I claim pension under the general law
on account of disease of eyes
as a result of smallpox
contracted in service—

The varicose veins came on both my legs
soon after the war and the sores were there
when I first put in my claim—

I claim pension for rheumatism
and got my toe broke and I was struck
in the side with the breech of a gun
breaking my ribs—

I was a man stout and healthy
over 27 years of age when I enlisted—

When I enlisted I had a little mustache,
and some chin whiskers—

I was a green boy right off the farm and did
just what I was told to do—

When I went to enlist the recruiting officer
said to me, your name is John Wilson.
I said, no, my name is Robert Harrison,
but he put me down as John Wilson. I was
known while in service by that name—

I cannot read nor write, and I do not know
how my name was spelled when I enlisted
nor do I know how it is spelled now
I always signed my name while in the army
by making my mark
I know my name by sound—

My mother said after my discharge that the reason
the officer put my name down as John Wilson
was he could draw my bounty—

I am the son of Solomon and Lucinda Sibley——

I am the only living child of Dennis Campbell——

My father was George Jourdan and my mother was Millie Jourdan——

My mother told me that John Barnett was my father——

My mother was Mary Eliza Jackson and my father Reuben Jackson——

My name on the roll was Frank Nunn. No sir,
it was not Frank Nearn——

My full name is Dick Lewis Barnett.
I am the applicant for pension
on account of having served
under the name Lewis Smith
which was the name I wore before
the days of slavery were over——

My correct name is Hiram Kirkland.
Some persons call me Harry and others call me Henry,
but neither is my correct name.

GHAZAL

The sky is a dry pitiless white. The wide rows stretch on into death.
Like famished birds, my hands strip each stalk of its stolen crop: our name.

History is a ship forever setting sail. On either shore: mountains of men,
Oceans of bone, an engine whose teeth shred all that is not our name.

Can you imagine what will sound from us, what we'll rend and claim
When we find ourselves alone with all we've ever sought: our name?

Or perhaps what we seek lives outside of speech, like a tribe of goats
On a mountain above a lake, whose hooves nick away at rock. Our name

Is blown from tree to tree, scattered by the breeze. Who am I to say what,
In that marriage, is lost? For all I know, the grass has caught our name.

Having risen from moan to growl, growl to a hound's low bray,
The voices catch. No priest, no sinner has yet been taught our name.

Will it thunder up, the call of time? Or lie quiet as bedrock beneath
Our feet? Our name our name our name our fraught, fraught name.

III.

THE UNITED STATES WELCOMES YOU

Why and by whose power were you sent?

What do you see that you may wish to steal?

Why this dancing? Why do your dark bodies

Drink up all the light? What are you demanding

That we feel? Have you stolen something? Then

What is that leaping in your chest? What is

The nature of your mission? Do you seek

To offer a confession? Have you anything to do

With others brought by us to harm? Then

Why are you afraid? And why do you invade

Our night, hands raised, eyes wide, mute

As ghosts? Is there something you wish to confess?

Is this some enigmatic type of test? What if we

Fail? How and to whom do we address our appeal?

NEW ROAD STATION

History is in a hurry. It moves like a woman
Corralling her children onto a crowded bus.

History spits *Go, go, go,* lurching at the horizon,
Hammering the driver's headrest with her fist.

Nothing else moves. The flies settle in place
Watching with their million eyes, never bored.

The crows strike their bargain with the breeze.
They cluck and caw at the women in their frenzy,

The ones who suck their teeth, whose skirts
Are bathed in mud. But history is not a woman,

And it is not the crowd forming in a square.
It is not the bright swarm of voices chanting *No*

And *Now*, or even the rapt silence of a room
Where a film of history is right now being screened.

Perhaps history is the bus that will only wait so long
Before cranking its engine to barrel down

The road. Maybe it is the voice coming in
Through the radio like a long-distance call.

Or the child in the crook of his mother's arm
Who believes history must sleep inside a tomb,

Or the belly of a bomb.

THEATRICAL IMPROVISATION

Finally, a woman stands. Her body tightens.
She wrings her hands. *At first, I didn't think*
I heard it. Then I saw his face and understood.
I was pulled and dragged.

And another:
I was dragged and choked.

And another:
A woman yanked mine from my head and told me
It was no longer allowed.

A man hawks,
Pretends to spit. *We want these people*
To feel unwanted. We want them
To feel that everything around them is
Against them. He puts a hand on his hip.
And we want them to be afraid. His free hand
Hangs in the air to his side as if steadied
By a tall stick, or a rifle with its butt end
On the ground.

And a beat. Strange weather
Moves across each face. The women pass
From fright to rage. They circle him,
Closing in.

He, too, is changed, steps back,
Drops. *I was asleep outside—it was warm enough*
To sleep outside the station. They didn't know me,
I didn't know them. I woke to their piss in my face.
Then they hit me with a metal rod. They broke my
Fingers, cracked some of my ribs.

They fidget
Over him like rowdies, then crouch down,
Level with his eyes: *The only way this country's*
Going to turn around is—

     It will be a bloodbath—

Tell him!—

   And it will be a nasty, messy motherfucker.

The one stands slowly up. The four
High-five and sprint away.

     The house
Is dark and not half full. There is a collective
Clenching in the chest.

    A new actor shifts
From foot to foot. Cowers in the light.
Foreign workers gave us paper and told us to draw.
Some of us drew families fleeing. Some of us drew
Helicopters in the sky and our houses below burning.
Some of us drew men pointing guns at each other.
Some drew boats about to go under. Some filled
The page with angry water. Some drew our mothers
And our older sisters kicking their legs and grabbing
At air when they got pulled away by the hair. He
Stays there, gaze directed nowhere.

      Others come.
The line of actors stretches past the wings, out
Into the street. Some with voices, some whose
Bodies speak, each dragging something dark,
Perceptible. A burden given or chosen. Even
The empty, the bereft—they're saddled
With it, can't without assistance put it down.

One, black, slim, a boy himself, stands beside
The child.

        Another, broad, solid as granite,
Sputters into sudden tears.

A woman, white-haired, shuffles almost to him,
But stops, turns back.

          A fat man in a suit, stooped,
Can still command his arms to flail as he rails *Them!*
Them and them and them and them and them!

Among viewers, there is the dawning sense
That this is mere rehearsal, that the performance
Has not yet been contracted, nor scheduled,
Nor agreed upon, nor even cast.

            Back of the house,
A single person claps.

        Then erupts a panicked
Applause that doesn't know how to end.

UNREST IN BATON ROUGE

after the photo by Jonathan Bachman

Our bodies run with ink dark blood.
Blood pools in the pavement's seams.

Is it strange to say love is a language
Few practice, but all, or near all speak?

Even the men in black armor, the ones
Jangling handcuffs and keys, what else

Are they so buffered against, if not love's blade
Sizing up the heart's familiar meat?

We watch and grieve. We sleep, stir, eat.
Love: the heart sliced open, gutted, clean.

Love: naked almost in the everlasting street,
Skirt lifted by a different kind of breeze.

WATERSHED

200 cows   more than 600 hilly acres

     property would have been even larger
had J not sold 66 acres to DuPont for
     waste from its Washington Works factory
where J was employed
         did not want to sell
     but needed money   poor health
mysterious ailments

Not long after the sale cattle began to act
deranged
     footage shot on a camcorder
grainy   intercut with static
Images jump repeat   sound accelerates
  slows down
     quality of a horror movie

the rippling shallow water   the white ash
  trees shedding their leaves
        a large pipe
discharging green water
       a skinny red cow
hair missing   back humped

a dead black calf in snow   its eye
  a brilliant chemical blue

       a calf's bisected head
liver   heart   stomachs   kidneys
    gall bladder   some dark   some green

cows with stringy tails   malformed hooves
    lesions   red receded eyes   suffering   slobbering
       staggering like drunks

It don't look like
        anything I've been into before

I began rising through the ceiling of each floor in the hospital as though I were being pulled by some force outside my own volition. I continued rising until I passed through the roof itself and found myself in the sky. I began to move much more quickly past the mountain range near the hospital and over the city. I was swept away by some unknown force, and started to move at an enormous speed. Just moving like a thunderbolt through a darkness.

R's taking on the case I found to be inconceivable

It just felt like the right thing to do
                      a great
opportunity to use my background for people who
           really needed it

R: filed a federal suit
            pulled permits
            land deeds
                a letter that mentioned
a substance at the landfill
           PFOA
        perfluorooctanoic acid

a soap-like agent used in
           Scotchgard™
                Teflon™

PFOA: was to be incinerated or
                     sent to chemical waste facilities
                          not to be flushed into water or sewers

DuPont:
               pumped hundreds of thousands of pounds
                    into the Ohio River
               dumped tons of PFOA sludge
                    into open unlined pits

PFOA:
          increased the size of the liver in rats and rabbits
                    results replicated in dogs
          caused birth defects in rats
          caused cancerous testicular pancreatic and
                    liver tumors in lab animals
          possible DNA damage from exposure
          bound to plasma proteins in blood
          was found circulating through each organ
          high concentrations in the blood of factory workers
          children of pregnant employees had eye defects
          dust vented from factory chimneys settled well-beyond
                    the property line
          entered the water table
          concentration in drinking water 3x international safety limit
          study of workers linked exposure with prostate cancer
          worth $1 billion in annual profit

It don't look like anything I've been into before

*Every individual thing glowed with life. Bands of energy were being dispersed from
a huge universal heartbeat, faster than a raging river. I found I could move as fast
as I could think.*

DuPont:

       did not make this information public

       declined to disclose this finding

       considered switching to new compound that appeared less toxic

           and stayed in the body for a much shorter duration of time

       decided against it

       decided it needed to find a landfill for toxic sludge

       bought 66 acres from a low-level employee

           at the Washington Works facility

J needed money

           had been in poor health

a dead black calf

           its eye chemical blue

cows slobbering

           staggering like drunks

I could perceive the Earth, outer space, and humanity from a spacious and indescribable "God's eye view." I saw a planet to my left covered with vegetation of many colors, no signs of mankind or any familiar shorelines. The waters were living waters, the grass was living, the trees and the animals were more alive than on earth.

D's first husband had been a chemist

           When you

worked at DuPont in this town you could have

everything you wanted

           DuPont paid for his education

secured him a mortgage   paid a generous salary

even gave him a free supply of PFOA

He explained that the planet we call Earth really has a proper name, has its own energy, is a true living being, was very strong but has been weakened considerably.

                                            which she used

as soap in the family's dishwasher

I could feel Earth's desperate situation. Her aura appeared to be very strange, made me wonder if it was radioactivity. It was bleak, faded in color, and its sound was heart wrenching.

                                        Sometimes

her husband came home sick—fever, nausea, diarrhea, vomiting—"Teflon flu"

      an emergency hysterectomy

                          a second surgery

I could tell the doctor everything he did upon my arrival down to the minute details of accompanying the nurse to the basement of the hospital to get the plasma for me; everything he did while also being instructed and shown around in Heaven.

Clients called R to say they had received diagnoses of cancer
       or that a family member had died

       W who had cancer had died of a heart attack

       Two years later W's wife died of cancer

They knew this stuff was harmful
       and they put it in the water anyway

I suspect that Earth may be a place of education.

PFOA detected in:
        American blood banks
        blood or vital organs of:
                Atlantic salmon
                swordfish
                striped mullet
                gray seals
                common cormorants
                Alaskan polar bears
                brown pelicans
                sea turtles
                sea eagles
                California sea lions
                Laysan albatrosses on a
                    wildlife refuge in the
                    middle of the North
                    Pacific Ocean

Viewing the myriad human faces with an incredible, intimate, and profound love.
This love was all around me, it was everywhere, but at the same time it was also me.

        We see a situation

    that has gone

        from Washington Works

All that was important in life was the love we felt.

to statewide

All that was made, said, done, or even thought without love was undone.

to everywhere

it's global

In my particular case, God took the form of a luminous warm water. It does not mean that a luminous warm water is God. It is just that, for me, it was experiencing the luminous warm water that I felt the most connection with the eternal.

POLITICAL POEM

If those mowers were each to stop
      at the whim, say, of a greedy thought,
   and then the one off to the left

were to let his arm float up, stirring
      the air with that wide, slow, underwater
   gesture meaning *Hello!* and *You there!*

aimed at the one more than a mile away
      to the right. And if he in his work were to pause,
   catching that call by sheer wish, and send

back his own slow one-armed dance,
      meaning *Yes!* and *Here!* as if threaded
   to a single long nerve, before remembering

his tool and shearing another message
      into the earth, letting who can say how long
   graze past until another thought, or just the need to know,

might make him stop and look up again at the other,
      raising his arm as if to say something like *Still?*
   and *Oh!* and then to catch the flicker of joy

rise up along those other legs and flare
      into another bright *Yes!* that sways a moment
   in the darkening air, their work would carry them

into the better part of evening, each mowing
      ahead and doubling back, then looking up to catch
   sight of his echo, sought and held

in that instant of common understanding,
　　　　the *God* and *Speed* of it coming out only after
　　both have turned back to face to the sea of *Yet*

and *Slow.* If they could, and if what glimmered
　　　　like a fish were to dart back and forth across
　　that wide wordless distance, the day, though gone,

would never know the ache of being done.
　　　　If they thought to, or would, or even half-wanted,
　　their work—the humming human engines

pushed across the grass, and the grass, blade
　　　　after blade, assenting—would take forever.
　　But I love how long it would last.

IV.

ETERNITY

Landscape Painting

It is as if I can almost still remember.
As if I once perhaps belonged here.

The mountains a deep heavy green, and
The rocky steep drop to the waters below.

The peaked roofs, the white-plastered
Brick. A clothesline in a neighbor's yard

Made of sticks. The stone path skimming
The ridge. A ladder asleep against a house.

What is the soul allowed to keep? Every
Birth, every small gift, every ache? I know

I have knelt just here, torn apart by loss. Lazed
On this grass, counting joys like trees: cypress,

Blue fir, dogwood, cherry. Ageless, constant,
Growing down into earth and up into history.

———————

Lama Temple

It was a shock to be allowed in, for once
Not held back by a painted iron fence.

And to take it in with just my eyes (*No Photos*
Signs were discreet, yet emphatic). Coins,

Bills on a tray. Two women and then a man
Bowed before a statue to pray. Outside

Above the gates, a sprung balloon
And three kites swam east on a high fast

Current. And something about a bird
Flapping hard as it crossed my line of sight—

The bliss it seemed to make and ride without
Ever once gliding or slowing—the picture of it

Meant, suddenly, *youth*, and I couldn't help it,
I had to look away.

———————

Nanluoguxiang Alley

Every chance I get, every face I see, I find myself
Searching for a glimpse of myself, my daughter, my sons.

More often, I find there former students, old lovers,
Friends I knew once and had until now forgotten. My

Sisters, a Russian neighbor, a red-haired American actor.
And on and on, uncannily, as though all of us must be

Buried deep within each other.

———————

Songzhuang Art Village

You pull canvases from racks: red daisies,
Peonies in a blue vase, an urn of lilies

Like spirits flown from the dead. A self-
Portrait in a white dress, faceless but for one eye,

And all around you what could be empty
Coffins or guitar cases, or dark leaves

On a swirling sea. On a column in a black frame
Hangs a photo of your mother, a smiling

Girl in an army coat. *Can any of us save ourselves*,
You once wrote, *save another?* Below her,

All beard, practically, and crevassed brow,
Tolstoy stares in the direction of what once

Must have seemed the future.

———————

Mutianyu, Great Wall

Farther ahead, another tourist loses his footing
And grabs hold of a brick,

                   which comes off
In his hand, crumbles where it lands.

ASH

Strange house we must keep and fill.

House that eats and pleads and kills.

House on legs. House on fire. House infested

With desire. Haunted house. Lonely house.

House of trick and suck and shrug.

Give-it-to-me house. *I-need-you-baby* house.

House whose rooms are pooled with blood.

House with hands. House of guilt. House

That other houses built. House of lies

And pride and bone. House afraid to be alone.

House like an engine that churns and stalls.

House with skin and hair for walls.

House the seasons singe and douse.

House that believes it is not a house.

BEATIFIC

I watch him bob across the intersection,
Squat legs bowed in black sweatpants.

I watch him smile at nobody, at our traffic
Stopped to accommodate his slow going.

His arms churn the air. His comic jog
Carries him nowhere. But it is as if he hears

A voice in our idling engines, calling him
Lithe, *Swift*, *Prince of Creation*. Every least leaf

Shivers in the sun, while we sit, bothered,
Late, captive to this thing commanding

Wait for this man. Wait for him.

CHARITY

She is like a squat old machine,
Off-kilter but still chugging along
The uphill stretch of sidewalk
On Harrison Street, handbag slung
Crosswise and, I'm guessing, heavy.
And oh, the set of her face, her brow's
Profound tracks, her mouth cinched,
Lips pressed flat. Watching her
Bend forward to tussle with gravity,
Watching the berth she allows each
Foot (as if one is not on civil
Terms with the other), watching
Her shoulders braced as if lashed
By step after step after step, and
Her eyes' determination not to
Shift, or blink, or rise, I think:
I am you, one day out of five,
Tired, empty, hating what I carry
But afraid to lay it down, stingy,
Angry, doing violence to others
By the sheer freight of my gloom,
Halfway home, wanting to stop, to quit
But keeping going mostly out of spite.

IN YOUR CONDITION

That whole time away, I stayed dizzy. Everywhere,

Meats whirled round in a pit. Waiters crashed in

And out like the tide with trays and trays of fish.

Every chance, I slept: in the bathroom between courses,

A whole half-hour laid out like a corpse atop the bed.

I saw the beach from a castle in the hills. I climbed there

On Sunday carrying my purse, snapping the same pictures

From the year before, to be polite. Windows that belonged

To the queen maintain their perfect shape, though the glass

She would have paced behind is gone. Grass spreads

Like intrigue where once were rugs, and a double metal rail

Suggests a wall. Along a hall and up slick winding steps,

There was a view down into the valley, but I couldn't linger.

The baby kept me queasy, hungry, made my dress hike up

Though I was only eight weeks in. At a tavern on my last night,

I had to stand outside to breathe. I ordered bottle after bottle

Of water, though the red wine shimmered like nectar.

Flying home, I snuck a wedge of brie, and wept

Through a movie starring Angelina Jolie.

4½

Morning finds her curled like a prawn

Around a stuffed blue Pegasus, or the smallest

Prawn-pink lion. Or else she's barging

Into my room, and leaning in close so

It's her hair I wake to—that coarse, dark

Heaven of knots and purple fluff. And

She's hungry, but first she has to pee—

"Pee! Pee!" she sings, hopping in place, trying

To staunch off the wild ravenous river

She carries, until I'm awake for real, saying

"Go! Go! Hurry before you wet the floor!"

And then she tries, and succeeds, or else stands

Bereft, relieved, as a pool trickles out

Around her feet. She's like an island

Made of rock, with one lone tree at the top

Of the only mountain. She's like the sole

Incongruous goat tethered to the tree,

Smiling almost as you approach, scraping

The ground with its horns, and then—

Lickety split—lurching hard, daring

The rope to snap. She's hungry. She wants

"Bread, toasted, with no skin." And enough butter

To write her name in. Or a bowl of cereal ("But

Not the noisy kind"). She wants a movie, or maybe

Just the tussle of her will against mine,

That scrape and crack. Horn on rock. Rope

Relenting one fiber at a time. "I want that," she says,

Punctuating what she just said she wanted.

DUSK

What woke to war in me those years
When my daughter had first grown into
A solid self-centered self? I'd watch her
Sit at the table—well, not quite sit,
More like stand on one leg while
The other knee hovered just over the chair.
She wouldn't lower herself, as if
There might be a fire, or a great black
Blizzard of waves let loose in the kitchen,
And she'd need to make her escape. No,
She'd trust no one but herself, her own
New lean always jittering legs to carry her—
Where exactly? Where would a child go?
To there. There alone. She'd rest one elbow
On the table—the opposite one to the bent leg
Skimming the solid expensive tasteful chair.
And even though we were together, her eyes
Would go half-dome, shades dropped
Like a screen at some cinema the old aren't
Let into. I thought I'd have more time! I thought
My body would have taken longer going
About the inevitable feat of repelling her,
But now, I could see even in what food
She left untouched, food I'd bought and made
And all but ferried to her lips, I could see
How it smacked of all that had grown slack
And loose in me. Her other arm
Would wave the fork around just above
The surface of the plate, casting about
For the least possible morsel, the tiniest
Grain of unseasoned rice. She'd dip
Into the food like one of those shoddy
Metal claws poised over a valley of rubber
Bouncing balls, the kind that lifts nothing

Or next to nothing and drops it in the chute.
The narrow untouched hips. The shoulders
Still so naïve as to stand squared, erect,
Impervious facing the window open
Onto the darkening dusk.

URBAN YOUTH

You'd wake me for Saturday cartoons
When you were twelve and I was two.
Hong Kong Phooey, Fat Albert & *the Cosby Kids.*
In the '70s, everything shone bright as brass.

When you were twelve and I was two,
It was always autumn. Blue sky, flimsy clouds.
This was the '70s. Every bright day a brass
Trombone slept, leaning in your room.

Autumn-crisp air. Blue skies. Clouds
Of steam clotted the window near the stove (and
Slept in the trombone kept in your room). You
Wrote a poem about the sea and never forgot it.

Steam clotted the window near the stove
Where Mom stood sometimes staring out.
I forget now what there was to see.
So much now gone was only then beginning.

Mom stood once looking out while you and
Dad and Mike taught me to ride a two-wheeler.
So much was only then beginning. Should
I have been afraid? The hedges hummed with bees,

But it was you and Dad and Mike teaching me to ride,
Running along beside until you didn't have to hold on.
Who was afraid? The hedges thrummed with bees
That only sang. Every happy thing I've known,

You held, or ran alongside not having to hold.

THE EVERLASTING SELF

Comes in from a downpour

Shaking water in every direction—

A collaborative condition:

Gathered, shed, spread, then

Forgotten, reabsorbed. Like love

From a lifetime ago, and mud

A dog has tracked across the floor.

ANNUNCIATION

I feel ashamed, finally,

Of our magnificent paved roads,

Our bridges slung with steel,

Our vivid glass, our tantalizing lights,

Everything enhanced, rehearsed,

A trick. I've turned old. I ache most

To be confronted by the real,

By the cold, the pitiless, the bleak.

By the red fox crossing a field

After snow, by the broad shadow

Scraping past overhead.

My young son, eyes set

At an indeterminate distance,

Ears locked, tuned inward, caught

In some music only he has ever heard.

Not our cars, our electronic haze.

Not the piddling bleats and pings

That cause some hearts to race.

Ashamed. Like a pebble, hard

And small, hoping only to be ground to dust

By something large and strange and cruel.

REFUGE

Until I can understand why you
Fled, why you are willing to bleed,
Why you deserve what I must be
Willing to cede, let me imagine
You are my mother in Montgomery,
Alabama, walking to campus
Rather than riding the bus. I know
What they call you, what they
Try to convince you you lack.
I know your tired ankles, the sudden
Thunder of your laugh. Until
I want to give you what I myself deserve,
Let me love you by loving her.

Your sister in a camp in Turkey,
Sixteen, deserving of everything:
Let her be my daughter, who has
Curled her neat hands into fists,
Insisting nothing is fair and I
Have never loved her. Naomi,
Lips set in a scowl, young heart
Ransacking its cell. Let me lend
Her passion to your sister, and
Love her for her living rage, her
Need for *more*, and *now*, and *all*.
Let me leap from sleep if her voice
Sounds out, afraid, from down the hall.

I have seen men like your father
Walking up Harrison Street
Now that the days are getting longer.
Let me love them as I love my own
Father, whom I phoned once
From a valley in my life

To say what I feared I'd never
Adequately said, voice choked,
Stalled, hearing the silence spread
Around us like weather. What
Would it cost me to say it now,
To a stranger's father, walking home
To our separate lives together?

AN OLD STORY

We were made to understand it would be
Terrible. Every small want, every niggling urge,
Every hate swollen to a kind of epic wind.

Livid, the land, and ravaged, like a rageful
Dream. The worst in us having taken over
And broken the rest utterly down.

                              A long age
Passed. When at last we knew how little
Would survive us—how little we had mended

Or built that was not now lost—something
Large and old awoke. And then our singing
Brought on a different manner of weather.

Then animals long believed gone crept down
From trees. We took new stock of one another.
We wept to be reminded of such color.

NOTES

"Hill Country" is for Bill Johnson.

"Declaration" is an erasure poem drawn from the text of the Declaration of Independence.

"The Greatest Personal Privation" and "Unwritten" are for Nan and Erskine Clarke. Both are erasure poems drawn from correspondence between members of the Mary and Charles Colcock Jones family regarding the sale of slaves Patience, Porter, and their children, members of the Geechee/Gullah communities in Liberty County, Georgia. Early in his career as a Presbyterian minister, Jones contemplated supporting the abolition of slavery; he chose, instead, to work as a missionary and reformer in Liberty County, though he remained a slaveholder until his death in 1863. The history of the Joneses, and those enslaved on their plantations, is addressed in Erskine Clarke's *Dwelling Place: A Plantation Epic* (Yale University Press, 2005).

The text for "I Will Tell You the Truth about This, I Will Tell You All about It" is composed entirely of letters and statements of African Americans enlisted in the Civil War, and those of their wives, widows, parents, and children. While the primary documents in question have been abridged, the poem preserves the original spellings and punctuation to the extent possible throughout.

I relied upon the following books in composing the poem:

Regosin, Elizabeth A., and Donald R. Shaffer, eds. *Voices of Emancipation: Understanding Slavery, the Civil War, and Reconstruction through the U.S. Pension Bureau Files.* New York: New York University Press, 2008.

Berlin, Ira, and Leslie S. Rowland, eds. *Families and Freedom: A Documentary History of African-American Kinship in the Civil War Era.* New York: The New Press, 1997.

Once I began reading these texts, it became clear to me that the voices in question should command all of the space within my poem. I hope that they have been arranged in such a way as to highlight certain of the main factors affecting blacks during the Civil War, chiefly: the compound effects of slavery and war upon the African American family; the injustices to which black soldiers were often subject; the difficulty black soldiers and their widows faced in attempting to claim pensions after the war; and the persistence, good faith, dignity, and commitment to the ideals of democracy that ran through the many appeals to President Lincoln, the Freedmen's Bureau, and other authorities to whom petitions were routinely addressed during and after the war. Original sources are as follows:

November 21, 1864: Letter from Mrs. Jane Welcome to Abraham Lincoln

September 3, 1864: Letter from Spotswood Rice to his daughters

November 26, 1864: Affidavit of Joseph Miller

August 12, 1865: Letter from Norman Riley to Catherine Riley

August 25, 1864: Letter from Annie Davis to Abraham Lincoln

August 28, 1865: Letter from Catherine Riley to Norman Riley

December 7, 1866: Letter from Martin Lee to the head of the Freedmen's Bureau in Georgia.

March 9, 1867: Letter from Harrison Smith to his sister-in-law, Minta Smith

The long italicized sections of the poem are compiled of numerous sources. Stanza by stanza within each section, they are:

"Excellent Sir   My son went in the 54th regiment—":

Letter from Hannah Johnson to Abraham Lincoln, July 31, 1863

Letter from Rosanna Henson to Abraham Lincoln, July 11, 1864

Letter from Members of the 55th Massachusetts Infantry to Abraham Lincoln, July 16, 1864

Unsigned letter to General Sickels, Jan. 13, 1866

Letter from Hiram A. Peterson to his father, Aaron Peterson, Oct. 24, 1863

Letter from Hannah Johnson to Abraham Lincoln, July 31, 1863

Unsigned letter to General Sickels, Jan. 13, 1866

Letter from Hiram A. Peterson to Aaron Peterson, Oct. 24, 1863

Letter from Aaron Peterson to Secretary of War, Hon. Edwin M. Stanten, Oct. 29, 1863

Letter from James Herney to Secretary Stanten, May 15, 1866

Letter from Hannah Johnson to Abraham Lincoln, July 31, 1863

Letter from Hiram A. Peterson to Aaron Peterson, Oct. 24, 1863

"I am 60 odd years of age——":

Deposition of Ellen Wade, Nov. 21, 1906, Civil War Pension File of Walker Bettlesworth (alias Wade), 116th USCI, RG 15

Deposition of Thomas W. Wilbourn, Apr. 14, 1909, Civil War Pension File of Thomas Wilbert (alias Thomas W. Wilbourn), 122nd USCI, RG 15

Deposition of Alice Bettlesworth (alias Wade), Nov. 21, 1906, Civil War Pension File of Walker Bettlesworth (alias Wade), 116th USCI, RG 15

Deposition of Charles Franklin Crosby, June 19, 1914, Civil War Pension File of Frank Nunn (alias Charles Franklin Crosby), 86th USCI, RG 15

Deposition of Emma Frederick, June 2, 1899, Civil War Pension file of Clement Frederick, 70th and 71st USCI, RG 15

Deposition of Hiram Kirkland, Nov. 26, 1902, Civil War Pension File of Hiram Kirkland, 101st and 110th USCI, RG 15

Deposition of Charles Washington, Dec. 18, 1905, Civil War Pension File of Charles Washington, 47th USCI, RG 15

Deposition of Emma Frederick, March 12, 1903

Deposition of Hiram Kirkland

Deposition of Emma Frederick, Apr. 11, 1903

Deposition of Thomas W. Wilbourn

Deposition of Charles Washington

Deposition of Alexander Porter, May 3, 1900, Civil War Pension File of Alexander Porter, 58th USCI, RG 15

Deposition of Hiram Kirkland

Deposition of Revel Garrison, Sept. 10, 1888, Civil War Pension File of Revel Garrison, 2nd USCC, RG 15

Affidavit of Benjamin Courtney, Apr. 28, 1908, Civil War Pension File of Benjamin Courtney, 51st USCI, RG 15

Deposition of Charles Washington

Deposition of Robert Harrison, Apr. 11, 1890, Civil War Pension File of Robert Harris (alias Robert Harrison, alias John Wilson), RG 15

Deposition of Robert Harrison

Affidavit of William L. Dickerson, Oct. 23, 1902, William L. Dickinson (alias Dixon, Dickson, and Dickerson), 14th USCI, RG 15

Deposition of Robert Harrison

Affidavit of Hannibal Sibley, Jan. 11, 1893, Civil War Pension File of Solomon Sibley, 63rd USCI, RG 15

Affidavit of Martin Campbell, June 10, 1889, Civil War Pension File of Dennis Campbell, 63rd USCI, RG 15

Deposition of Louis Jourdan, May 27, 1915, Civil War Pension File of Louis Jourdan, 77th USCI and 10th USCHA, RG 15

Deposition of Dick Lewis Barnett, May 17, 1911, Civil War Pension File of Lewis Smith (alias Dick Lewis Barnett), 77th USCI and 10th USCHA, RG 15

Deposition of Mary Jane Taylor, May 13, 1919, Civil War Pension File of Samuel Taylor, 45th USCI, RG 15

Deposition of Charles Franklin Crosby, June 19, 1914, Civil War Pension File of Frank Nunn (alias Charles Franklin Crosby), 86th USCI, RG 15

Deposition of Dick Lewis Barnett

Deposition of Hiram Kirkland

Italicized lines in "Theatrical Improvisation" quote from and are based upon the following real-life sources:

Reported attacks on Muslim American women in the days after the 2016 presidential election as collected by the Southern Poverty Law Center.

Comments by Andrew Anglin: "Fear. *Now is the time for it.* . . . We want these people to feel that everything around them is against them. And we want them to be afraid," from a November 10, 2016, post to neo-Nazi Daily Stormer website entitled "Female Hajis Fear to Wear the Headtowel in Public after Trump Win—You Should Yell at Them."

In 2015 fifty-eight-year-old Guillermo Rodriguez, a homeless Latino immigrant, was attacked while sleeping outside a Boston commuter rail station. One of his assailants, Scott Leader, told police the violence was acceptable because the victim was homeless and Hispanic. *Reuters*, May 17, 2016.

Comments by Patrick Stein, member of an antigovernment group called the Crusaders, who was arrested after allegedly finalizing plans to blow up an apartment complex housing more than 100 Somali-born, Muslim immigrants and a small mosque: "The only fucking way this country's ever going to get turned around is it will be a bloodbath and it will be a nasty, messy motherfucker. Unless a lot more people in this country wake up and smell the fucking coffee and decide they want this country back . . . we might be too late, if they do wake up . . . I think we can get it done. But it ain't going to be nothing nice about it," *United States of America, Plaintiff v. Curtis Wayne Allen, Patrick Eugene Stein, and Gavin Wayne Wright, Defendants.*

Exhibitions of artwork by refugee children from Sudan (2005) and Syria (2017).

"Watershed" is a found poem drawn from two sources: a *New York Times Magazine* January 6, 2016, article by Nathaniel Rich entitled, "The Lawyer Who Became DuPont's Worst Nightmare," and excerpts of the narratives of survivors of near-death experiences as catalogued on www.nderf.org.

"Eternity" is set in Beijing, China, and its environs. The poem's penultimate section is for Yi Lei.

ACKNOWLEDGMENTS

Grateful acknowledgment is made to the editors of the following journals, who first published versions of these poems: The Academy of American Poets' "Poem-a-Day," the *Awl*, the *Believer*, *Callaloo*, *Cave Wall*, the *Cortland Review*, *Harvard Review*, the *Nation*, the *New Yorker*, *Tin House*, and *TriQuarterly*.

"Garden of Eden" was the 2017 Commencement Poem of St. Francis College.

"Realm of Shades" appears in *Bearden's Odyssey: Poets Respond to the Art of Romare Bearden* (TriQuarterly Books, 2017).

"I Will Tell You the Truth about This, I Will Tell You All about It" was written to accompany the Civil War 150th exhibition at the Smithsonian Museum's National Portrait Gallery in 2011. It appears in the folio *Lines in Long Array: A Civil War Commemoration: Poems and Photographs, Past and Present* (Smithsonian Books, 2013).

"Ghazal" was written for *The Ecstasy of St. Kara: Kara Walker, New Work* (The Cleveland Museum of Art, 2016).

"New Road Station" was written for broadcast on the *All Things Considered* "News Poet" feature on National Public Radio.

"Unrest in Baton Rouge" was written for broadcast on WNYC's *Studio 360*.

"Urban Youth" is for Conrad.

"Annunciation" appears in Liverpool Presents Sgt Pepper at 50 for the city's celebration May 25 to June 16, 2017.

"Refuge" was written as the closing statement to the conference "Seeking Refuge: Faith-Based Approaches to Forced Migration," which took place at Princeton University on March 3 and 4, 2017.

TRACY K. SMITH is the author of three previous books of poetry: *The Body's Question*, winner of the Cave Canem Poetry Prize; *Duende*, winner of the James Laughlin Award of the Academy of American Poets; and *Life on Mars*, winner of the Pulitzer Prize. She is also the editor of an anthology, *American Journal: Fifty Poems for Our Time*, and the author of a memoir, *Ordinary Light*, which was named a finalist for the National Book Award. Other honors include a Wallace Stegner Fellowship, a Rona Jaffe Foundation Writers' Award, a Whiting Writers' Award, and an Academy of American Poets Fellowship. In 2017, Smith was appointed Poet Laureate of the United States. She is the Roger S. Berlind '52 Professor of the Humanities and Director and Professor of Creative Writing at Princeton University, and lives in Princeton, New Jersey, with her family.

The text of *Wade in the Water* is set in Perpetua. Book design and composition by Bookmobile Design and Digital Publisher Services, Minneapolis, Minnesota. Manufactured by Versa Press on acid-free, 30 percent post-consumer wastepaper.